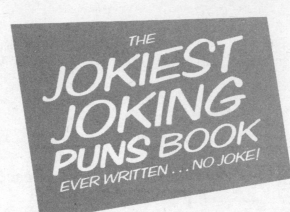

THE
JOKIEST
JOKING
PUNS BOOK
EVER WRITTEN . . . NO JOKE!

LOOKING FOR MORE JOKES TO IMPRESS YOUR FRIENDS AND
BUILD YOUR ULTIMATE JOKEMASTER COLLECTION?

YOU'LL LOVE...

THE JOKIEST JOKING JOKE BOOK EVER WRITTEN...NO JOKE!

***THE JOKIEST JOKING KNOCK-KNOCK JOKE BOOK
EVER WRITTEN...NO JOKE!***

THE JOKIEST JOKING TRIVIA BOOK EVER WRITTEN...NO JOKE!

***THE JOKIEST JOKING BATHROOM JOKE BOOK
EVER WRITTEN...NO JOKE!***

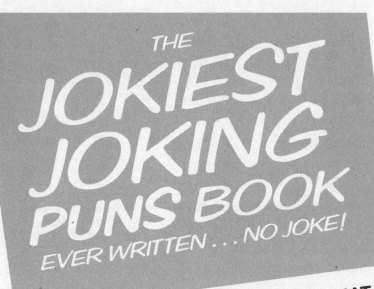

THE JOKIEST JOKING PUNS BOOK EVER WRITTEN ... NO JOKE!

1,001 BRAND-NEW WISECRACKS THAT WILL KEEP YOU LAUGHING OUT LOUD

Jokes by Brian Boone

Illustrations by Amanda Brack

CASTLE POINT BOOKS

NEW YORK

ISBN 978-1-250-20199-7 (trade paperback)

ISBN 978-1-250-20222-2 (ebook)

Our books may be purchased in bulk for promotional, educational, or business use. Please contact your local bookseller or the Macmillan Corporate and Premium Sales Department at 1-800-221-7945, extension 5442, or by email at MacmillanSpecialMarkets@macmillan.com.

First Edition: March 2019

10 9 8 7 6 5 4 3 2 1

To Megan and Brendan, who
both enjoy my jokes and try to
out-silly me with their own.

CONTENTS

INTRODUCING . . .

Does something in here sound funny to you? We sure hope so, because we love silly puns so much that we put together this book of more than 1,000 of the best puns of all time. Presenting: *The Jokiest Joking Puns Book Ever Written . . . No Joke!*

But just what *is* a pun, exactly? Well, call us a grounded aircraft, because we can . . . ex-plane. (Ha!) A pun is a joke that results from a clever twist of words, or a tweak of a phrase, or playing off the fact that one word sounds an awful lot like another word. The result: It ought to make you laugh . . . or groan.

Try this one out: What's the difference between a piano and a tuna? Well, you can tune a piano . . . but you can't tuna fish! Get it? (We know you did . . . we can hear you laughing *and* groaning.)

Your friends, family, and classmates will love it when you brighten their day with one of these ridiculous, puntastic, puntactular, joke-ular jokes that are so packed with laughs they're huge-arious! We really think this is one . . . for the books!

Ready for some fun in the pun? Turn the page! (Or, if you're reading this at a library . . . check it out! Hey, once you get started telling puns, it's hard to stop.)

1
CREATURE FEATURE

**A teddy bear is a stuffed animal,
and this chapter is animal-stuffed.**

What do you call an alligator who wears a vest?
An investigator.

If you really need to get in touch with a fish,
the best way to communicate is to drop them a line.

It isn't a snail's heavy shell that makes it
move so slow. In fact, scientists have
carefully removed the shell
to see if they'd be faster,

but if anything, it made them sluggish.

Two silkworms had a race,

but they ultimately ended in a tie.

A dog was arrested for giving birth on the side
of the road.

Police charged her with littering.

What do you call a dinosaur whose vision is based on movement?

A do-ya-think-it-saw-us.

The farmer needed to move to a new farm, and he couldn't fit all the cows in one van,

so he called a moooooving company.

That baby bird looks just like her father.

She's a real chirp off the old block!

Why are there always ducks on the pond, no matter how early you go? Because they always rise at the quack of dawn.

Cows have to buy their cowbells and grass somewhere.

That's why they read a lot of cattle-logs.

Never, ever tell a pig your deepest, darkest secret.

They're bound to squeal!

You'd think clowns would be worried about sharing the circus with lions, but lions don't eat clowns.

You see, a lion tried to eat a clown once.
He spit them out because it tasted funny.

Did you know that there's a surefire way to catch a whole school of fish at once?

Just use some bookworms.

Every day around noon, young cows like to eat their lunch together.

They do it in the calf-eteria.

A dinosaur crashed his car.

Talk about a tyrannosaurus wrecks!

Did you know that dragons are nocturnal animals?

They sleep all day so that they can fight knights.

Squirrels will usually run away from people, so how do you get one to like you?

Just act like you're nuts!

All the horses that lived next to each other in their stables were all very friendly.

It was a lovely neigh-borhood.

-ZZZZZ

An awake dinosaur is a dinosaur.
A sleeping dinosaur is a dinosnore.

They say that it's impossible to make an octopus laugh, but it's just not true.

You have to tickle them ten times . . . ten tickles.

A puppy had never sat on sandpaper before.

When asked to describe it, she said it was "ruff."

What dinosaur knows the most words?

The thesaurus.

There was once a pony who was said to be a fantastic singer. But when she finally took the stage, she discovered she was a little hoarse.

Why do bees have such sticky hair?
They use a honeycomb.

A farmer thought he had a really great dairy cow, but it produced no milk.
Talk about an udder failure.

Coral are sea creatures, but they do get stressed out.
Mostly over current events.

Why are cats good at stirring?
They bring their own whiskers.

The sheepdog counted 30 sheep, but the farmer only counted 28.
Why the difference?
The dog rounded them up.

Never play checkers with the world's fastest cat.
He's a cheetah!

Did you hear that the frog left his car illegally parked?
It got toad away.

Did you see that film about dairy cows?

I don't think I've ever seen a better moooovie.

**A dolphin strapped on a huge fake fin
and swam near the beach just to scare people.**

It could do a killer whale impression.

What do you call a snake that's 3.14159 feet long?

A pi-thon.

Why did the cowboy buy a Dachshund?
Because he wanted to get a long, little doggy.

A dog lost her tail, so she got a new one at the *retail* store.

Some fuzzy aquatic mammals escaped from the zoo.
It was otter chaos!

Dad: There are moose falling from the sky!
Mom: It's just reindeer.

Did you hear about the cat who ate nothing but lemons? What a sourpuss!

The chicken leg approached its old nemesis, the beef steak.
"So, we meat again."

What's the difference between bird flu and swine flu, anyway?
One needs tweetment and the other needs an oinkment.

The champion race horse was made completely out of dough.
After all, it was a pure bread.

The buffalo's son went off to college.
So she said, "Bison."

Why do ants not get sick?
Because they have little anty-bodies.

Why did the octopus beat the shark in a fight?
Because it was well-armed.

What do you call a really tall cow?
High steaks.

What do you call a bear with no teeth?
A gummy bear.

What kind of car does a sheep drive?

A Su-bah-ru.

Smaller babies may be delivered by stork because they're small.

If they're bigger, they need a crane.

Do you like pig puns?

Personally, I find them boaring.

How does a penguin build its house?

Igloos it together.

Teddy bears are the one animal that never gets hungry.
That's because they're always stuffed.

A fish walks into a restaurant. The waiter says, "Shouldn't you be in school?"

When will a horse talk?
Whinny wants to.

Did you see that horse that ate with its mouth open?
Such bad stable manners.

An elephant ate a bunch of 100-watt bulbs.
It wanted to have a light lunch.

What did the momma cow say to the baby cow?

"Come inside, it's pasture bedtime."

My cat sent me a letter in the mail.

She sent it furs class.

What do you call a horse and a bee that live next door to each other?

Neigh-buzz.

A crab got a great deal on a new sandcastle.
It only cost him a sand dollar!

What do you give an alligator that needs help?
Gator-aid.

What do you get when you cross a parrot and a caterpillar?
A walkie-talkie.

One cat scared another cat.
"Don't do that!" the victim said.
"You freaked meow!"

This pet store down the street is having a bird-sitting contest.
No perches necessary!

What's another name for a sleeping bull?
A bulldozer.

My poor cat just threw up on the carpet.
I don't think she's feline well.

A duck walked into a department store, grabbed some tiny duck shoes, and left.
As he went out the door, he said, "Put it on my bill."

A horse walked into a restaurant. The waiter said, "Hey,"
and the horse said, "Please!"

Some cats are great bowlers.
Such as alley cats.

An amoeba walked into a restaurant. The manager said,
"Come on in, but pay the tab before you split."

What do you call a bear stuck in the rain?
A drizzly bear.

Where do horses buy their clothes?

Old Neigh-vy.

Why wouldn't the chicken lay any eggs?

She was off the cluck.

Where do cats go to see fine art?

A mew-seum.

What do you get if you cross a dinosaur and a kangaroo? A tricera-hops.

Why are penguins so shy at parties?

They're nervous about breaking the ice.

How can a fish cut through wood?

With a sea-saw.

What's weirder than seeing a catfish?

Watching a fish bowl.

What do you call a dinosaur who wears a cowboy hats and boots? Tyrannosaurus Tex.

What should you do with a blue whale?

Well, try to cheer it up!

Did you hear about the feline that won a dog show?

It was an utter cat-astrophe!

Be careful when it's raining cats and dogs.

You don't want to step in a poodle.

What do you get when you cross a tortoise with a sheep? A turtleneck sweater.

Dogs go to obedience school, but young cats go to class, too.
Kittygarten!

One cat made fun of another cat until it cried. "I'm sorry," she said.
"I didn't mean to hurt your felines. I was only kitten."

Can hornets fly in the rain?
Only if they wear their yellow jackets.

How is a dog's tail like a cart?

They're both a-waggin'.

Why did the sheep go straight down the street without stopping?

There were no ewe turns allowed.

Where do rabbits go after they get married?

On their bunnymoon.

My friend, Mr. Alligator, couldn't make it to my birthday party.

He said he was swamped!

What does a mole read for fun?

The digtionary.

What kind of bug can tell time?

A clockroach.

What's another name for a nervous ant?

A jitterbug.

What kind of bee goes "mrmmrmrmrbzzzz"?

A mumblebee.

What's smarter than a talking bird?

A spelling bee.

Did you know that some pigs can do their own laundry?

It sounds like a bunch of hogwash!

You know you're near a chicken farm because of the fowl smell.

Fireflies will encourage each other to light up.

They'll often say to each other, "You glow, girl!"

What do you get if you cross a dog with a chicken?
A pooched egg.

A bee tried to enter a hive where he didn't belong.

A drone told him to mind his own buzzness.

A bunch of lice were really bugging me.

So I told them to get out of my hair.

Ants have antennae, but shouldn't those be called "ant-lers"?

How do you fix a broken baboon?

With a monkey wrench.

The cheetah down at the zoo had to get glasses. Why? It was seeing spots.

A bear walks up to a man and says, "Hello . . .
I am a bear."
The man replies, "Why the long pause?"
The bear replies, "I was born with these."

What animal asks the most questions?
A why-nocerous.

What do you call a bunny that issues parking tickets?
Meter Rabbit.

How do fish buy stuff?
With a credit cod.

Which dinosaur is the fastest?
The prontosaurus.

What dinosaur is the loudest at night?
The bronto-snore-us.

What's a dinosaur's favorite toy?
Tricera-tops.

What bird would you find at the end of a footrace?
The puffin.

How do you catch a baby frog?

With a toad pole.

What kind of lizards are comedians?

Stand-up chameleons.

Today is the tortoise's 100th birthday, so what should she and her friends do?

Shellebrate!

How do you wash a dog's hair?
With shampoodle.

Never believe anything a frog says.
They're am-fib-ians.

What do you get when you cross a swamp lizard with a pickle?
A croco-dill.

What do you call a cute but angry little monkey?
Furious George!

Why should you never insult an octopus?
You wouldn't want to hurt its feelers.

Do bees like classical music?
Sure—but only Bee-Thoven.

Why did the bee get a bank loan?
It wanted to open up a buzzness.

What's yellow, goes fast, and is full of shellfish?
A taxi crab.

How many skunks does it take to make a big stink?
A phew.

I once had a very funny cat.

She was very a-mews-ing.

Spiders must be so bored, because they're always climbing up the walls.

Have you ever been chased by a gang of rabbits?

It's a hare-owing experience.

Why do snakes make terrible soldiers?

They're unarmed.

Did you hear about the one-on-one giraffe race?

They were neck-and-neck the whole time.

Can a seagull eat 50 fish in an hour?

No, but a pelican.

What happens when you cross a pig with a bear?

You'd get a teddy boar.

The cat practiced its ballet routine over and over again.

Practice makes purrrrrfect.

Skunk friends text each other all the time.
They use their smell phones.

Did you hear about the pigs who wrote each other letters?
They were pen pals.

During the excitement of her wedding, the bride dropped her bouquet of flowers.
She exclaimed, "Whoopsie-daisies!"

What do you get when you cross a cow and a chicken?
A mooster!

Bees in love work harder at night.
Especially if they're on their honeymoon.

What clothes do fancy monkeys wear?
Dolce and Banana.

My shaggy dog got mad at me for forgetting to take him for a walk.
He was furryous!

Why wouldn't the hermit crab share its home?

It was shellfish.

Did you hear the one about the electric eel?

It's shocking!

The kid tried to annoy his brother by telling him bird puns. . . .

Until his brother realized that toucan play at that game.

When you read these jokes about athletes and athletics, you're bound to have a ball.

How do archers get in shape?
They do arrowbics!

Golfers always wear two pairs of pants when they're out on the links.
Just in case they get a hole in one.

Boxers have a very dangerous job. They constantly put themselves in arm's way.

Race car drivers are often very hungry.
It's because they skip brake fast.

With the way they use those wooden bats, baseball players are really just lumber-jocks.

What do you call it when two wrestlers join forces?
A clobberation.

When does a baseball game start?
In the big inning.

A lot of people think Rafael Nadal is a really good tennis player, but isn't Roger Federer?

What's the difference between a baseball player and a dog?
The baseball player gets a whole uniform. The dog only pants.

What do football stars and waffles have in common?
They're both made on the gridiron.

I used to know this really funny joke about a boomerang.
I forgot it, but I'm sure it will come back to me.

What basketball player smells the best?
The scenter!

The outdoors store was filled to the brim with people during its big paddle sale.

It was quite the oar deal.

A sports arena is a great place to spend a hot day.

It's full of fans.

That race car driver has had a very checkered past.

What kind of tea do hockey players drink?
Penal-tea.

Why are soccer players so good at math?

They know how to use their heads.

What do hockey players and magicians have in common?

Hat tricks!

What's a runner's favorite class?

Jog-raphy!

Where do tennis players like to live?

Volleywood!

Bungee jumping is an expensive sport.
Like they say, there's no such thing as a free lunge.

Why did the basketball player sit on the court and draw pictures of chickens?

She was trying to draw fowls.

What time did the basketball team chase the baseball team?

Five after nine.

Why is basketball so gross?

All the dribbling!

I didn't think I was going to like fencing, until I decided to take a stab at it.

I didn't think I was going to like soccer,
but as it turns out, I really get a kick out of it.

What do golfers wear on the links?
Tee-shirts.

If you're out camping and get cold, never build a fire in a kayak.
You can't have your kayak and heat it, too.

Skydivers chute first, ask questions later.
It's no wonder they're so well-grounded.

Why did the ballerina quit?
Because it was tutu hard.

Baseball is a team effort, especially those in the bullpen.

Everybody has to pitch inning.

People who do scuba.

Now there's a divers group of individuals.

I tried archery, but I didn't like it.

There were too many drawbacks.

A longshot was leading the big horse race, but not furlong.

Did you hear about the extremely indecisive rower?
He couldn't pick either oar.

A fishing pole is really just a fish stick.

How did the baseball player lose his house?
He made a home run.

When the coach called in a new pitcher, it was such a relief.

Have you ever thrown a spitball?
No, and I hope to never get invited to one either!

What do you get when insects play baseball?
Fly balls.

Why do they play baseball games at night?

Because bats sleep during the day.

What's the first thing that a ball does when it stops rolling?

It looks round.

First kid: Why is our tennis teacher so mad at you?

Second kid: He caught me raising a racquet.

What do you get when potatoes play baseball?
Fry balls.

What time does Serena Williams wake up each day?

Oh, ten-ish.

The bowling pins were tired of being mistreated.

So they went on strike.

What's the best time of year for jumping on a trampoline?

Spring!

Did you hear about the pig that joined the baseball team? She played snortstop.

We were going to tell you a joke about swimming, but it was too watered down.

Why shouldn't you ever play basketball with pigs?
Because they're ball hogs.

Cinderella was terrible at sports.
Probably because her coach was a pumpkin.

Did you hear about the ghost that joined the soccer team? It played ghoultender.

Cinderella was terrible at soccer.

She kept running away from the ball.

Do you want to hear a story about a basketball player?

It's a tall tale.

What did the football coach say to the broken vending machine?

"Give me my quarterback!"

Why are fish such terrible basketball players?
They're afraid of the net!

What got the martial artist so sick?

Kung flu.

Why didn't the dog like to wrestle?

Because she was a boxer.

A fish was arrested for swimming without a license. Police caught him and let him go.

That's when the fish said, "Whew, I'm off the hook!"

What exercise do swimmers do to get strong?
Pool-ups.

What's the difference between a baseball hit really high and a maggot's dad?

One's a pop fly, the other is a fly's pop.

What would you call a female goaltender standing between the two goal posts?

Annette.

What's the difference between a fisherman and a bad student?

One baits his hooks, the other hates his books.

Why are archers the best dressed of all the athletes?
They're always sporting bow ties.

Actual Names That Real People Have Given Their Boats

Vitamin Sea

Yacht to Be Working

Fah Get a Boat It

Costa Lotta

Seas the Day

Breakin' Wind

Your Place Oar Mine

A Crewed Interest

Bow Movement

Sea Me Smile

My Pride and Toy

Rest a Shore

Docked Wages

Seize the Bay

Fishfull Thinking

Weather Oar Knot

Nuclear Fishin'

Why did the athlete want to buy nine racquets?

Cause tennis too many.

A really bad gymnast walked into a bar.

Volleyball players can always make extra money.

It's customary to tip a good server.

What's a banker's favorite track and field event?

The vault.

On the bus on the way to the meet, the track team never stopped talking.

I guess they had a lot to discus.

How come sun tanning never caught on as a competitive sport?

Because the best you can ever get is bronze.

Yes, I'm competing in that stair-climbing competition.
Guess I better step up my game.

I lift weights only on Saturday and Sunday.
Monday to Friday are weak days.

Lately, my skiing skills are really going downhill.

A fisherman tried boxing, but he only threw hooks.

I think there are about two million or so baseball diamonds in the world.
But that's just a ballpark figure.

I know a lot of jokes about bad pole-vaulters.
But none of them seem to go over very well.

After hours of waiting for the bowling alley to open, we finally got the ball rolling.

I was overruled at the measuring competition.

The athlete claimed he long-jumped over 25 feet.
Actually his best jump only measured 23 feet.
This was a clear case of leap fraud.

Him: . . . and that's how they invented hockey.
Her: Icy.

Basketball players are always so well-rested.
You see, taller people sleep longer.

Did you hear about the Olympic speed skaters who refused to spend much money on their equipment?
Such cheapskates!

What's an NBA player's favorite TV drama?
The Mentallest.

You can't always be a Winter Olympics champion.
You win some, you luge some.

Did you hear they had to close down the ballpark because of an animal infestation?
The dugout was full of bats.

He wondered why the baseball off in the distance kept getting larger and larger.
And then, it hit him.

Never marry a tennis player.
Why not?
Because to them, love means nothing.

What's a boxer's favorite part of a joke?
The punchline!

3
WHERE ARE WE?

What's the most important thing for a bunch of jokes
about cities, countries, and places?
LOCATION! LOCATION! LOCATION!

Where do trees come from?
Oaklahoma.

Why'd they name it Wyoming?

Because wy not?

Did you know that Wisconsin has an unmarried daughter?

You can call her Miss Consin.

What's the heaviest state?
Mass-achusetts.

What state makes the most writing utensils?

Pencil-vania.

Did you know they made a sequel to Oregon?

It's called Moregon.

Did you hear the chocolate lover moved to Alaska?

He heard that it was full of mousse.

Lots of people want to visit the
Netherlands and buy clogs.
Wooden shoe?

What state is always the most prepared and best dressed for sports?

New Jersey.

Why is there only one Arizona?

Arizona room for the one.

If there were only three more states, we'd have 53.

And then we'd truly be one nation indivisible!

Why is England so wet?
The queen has had a long reign.

Did you hear that the Italian airline messed up and forgot to charge a plane full of passengers?
They were free to Rome!

What's the fastest-growing city in the world?
Dublin.

Did you know that England doesn't have any blood banks?
Sure, but at least it has a Liverpool.

Her: Do you really think I'm from South America?
Him: Yes, I Bolivia.

What's the most fast-paced city in the world?
Moscow. Everyone there is Russian.

What's the wealthiest city in Virginia?
Richmond.

Why is it called Washington, D.C.?
Because D C is just to the east.

There are so many lightning storms in Australia.
That's why they call it the land down thunder.

What's the oiliest place on Earth?

Greece.

What's the tallest building in your city?

The library, because it's got a lot of stories.

In which California city can you buy a really fancy Dodge Caravan?

Van Nuys.

Why are French goats so musically talented?
Because they're born with French horns.

Unless you visit Helsinki on your Scandinavian vacation, your trip remains un-Finnished.

When they told me La Paz was a capital city, I said, "I don't Bolivia."

Usually the only time CNN reports on anything in Norway it's Oslo news day.

Why are mountains the funniest place to visit?
Because they're hill areas!

Is there Nintendo in France?

Wii!

I went to a fancy English hotel.

Or, rather, a great Brit inn.

Where do the queen's dogs live?

In Barkingham Palace.

What state is great for dipping?

Oklahummus.

What state comes in a can packed with water?

Tunasee.

In what state would you find the most pigs?

New Hamshire.

Which state has excellent-smelling breath?

Vermint.

Which state is easiest to drive in?

Road Island.

When traveling to Central America, remember your manners.
Always say Belize and thank you.

I liked visiting Oceania, and I'd love to travel there Samoa.

What's the best way to talk to Vikings?
You better learn Norse Code.

She said she was from a country in the Middle East.

No, really, she's Syria's!

What's part of the United Kingdom and full of water?

Wales.

It would be fun to go the Emerald Isle.

Irish I could go this summer!

I can't wait to visit Africa.

I'm Ghana go later this year.

What state is the best to celebrate Thanksgiving in?
Kenturkey.

Want to go visit the most northern state?
Juneau you want to.
When I buy tickets, Alaska!

There's a giant country right above the United States.
Canada believe it?

I went to southeast Asia and it was so beautiful I felt weak Indonesia.

Cape Town Driver's License

S97347123
DOB
7/8/1996

Super Guy
100 Hero Street
Cape Town

Where do superheroes come from?
Cape Town.

What Dutch city is full of cute and fuzzy rodents?

Hamsterdam.

What makes up the city of Boston?

About two thousand bospounds.

Never play Hide and Seek with a mountain.

They always peak!

My grandparents went on vacation to Cuba.
I hear they're Havana good time.

What's a better name for a food court when you're on a diet?

A craveyard.

What kind of music might you hear in space?

Neptunes.

What's another name for a dentist's office?

A filling station.

Those two volcanoes over there are inseparable.
It's true lava!

What do you call a hug in Paris?

A French press.

Where do police officers like to eat?

At the arrestaurant.

A cruise ship is really just another name for a boatel.

Why are barns so noisy?

The goats have horns.

Where do astronauts get their astronaut training?
Mooniversity.

What stands overlooking New York and sneezes all day?

The A-Choo! of Liberty.

What European monument can't stand up?

The I-Fell Tower.

Where do termites go on vacation?

Hollywood!

Where do wasps go on vacation?

Stingapore.

Where do locks go on vacation?
Key West.

What's the world's laziest mountain?

Ever-rest.

What kind of hotels will birds stay in?

Anything cheep.

Where do shoelaces go on vacation?

Tie-land.

Where do ghosts go to relax?
The Boo-Hamas.

Where do shoes go on vacation?

Lace Vegas.

Where do pirates go on vacation?

Arrrrrrgentina.

What's the coldest place in South America?

Chile.

What do you call a bird stuck at the North Pole?
A brrrrrrrd.

Where do viruses go on vacation?

Germ-any.

In what state will you find the most lions?

Mane!

What's the most popular game show in the ocean?

Whale of Fortune.

What's the easiest kind of building to lift?
A lighthouse.

What state is full of cats and dogs and hamsters and gerbils?

Petsylvania.

Did you hear about the kid who ran all the way from New York to California?

He needed to West.

Why was the horse from Kentucky so generous to his horse friends?

Southern horspitality.

Where do zombies go for a swim?
The Dead Sea.

Did you hear about the cheese factory that exploded in France?

There was nothing but des brie.

Did you hear about the crime in the parking garage?

It was wrong on so many levels.

What planet is like a circus?

Saturn—it has three rings!

What's the most popular pop in the Midwest?

Mini-soda.

Where do ghosts go for a swim?
Lake Erie.

They may look far apart on a map, but Ireland is just one C away from Iceland.

If you want to live in Australia and eat eucalyptus leaves all day, you have to have the right koalifications.

Why is Tel Aviv a great vacation spot?
Because it Israeli fun there!

Her: I just climbed to the top of the world's biggest mountain.
Him: Wow, Everest?
Her: Sure, about every 100 feet or so.

Eating while traveling through Europe is very important.
Otherwise, when people get Hungary they're nothing Budapest.

There was a big historical event that rocked the Southern United States.
Many states witnessed it, and since they're so close to each other . . .
whatever Tennessee, Arkansas.

The Pacific Ocean met up with the Atlantic Ocean in Panama.

They didn't say anything—but they waved.

The Flintstones varies in popularity in the Middle East.

Not many people in Dubai like it, but the folks in Abu Dhabi do.

The best views in Paris are atop that famous tower.

You can certainly get an Eiffel!

I knew a guy who took a job in Seoul.

He thought it would be a good Korea move.

How come the astronaut never returned to the moon?
He wanted to give it some space.

A small area of undeveloped land may not seem like much.

But to me, it's a lot.

Kid: How come the moon was full the other day, but now it's just a crescent?

Mom: I wouldn't worry about it—it's just a phase.

I didn't used to want to visit that famous tower in Pisa.

But I think now I'm leaning toward it.

I went to a great concert in Hawaii.

The people were dancing in the isles!

4
TOM SWIFTIES

"Tom Swifties are a very old and very fun type of joke,"
the book's writer said authoritatively.

"I 'll go get the stick!" said Tom fetchingly.

"The number of people not attending class today really bothers me," said the teacher absent-mindedly.

"That *is* remarkable," remarked Tom.

"Have another cola," Tom coaxed.

"I enjoy hockey," said Tom puckishly.

"Want to play cards?" asked Tom ideally.

"I'm returning to school soon," said Tom with class.

"I'm going to give you a haircut!" said Tom barbarously.

"Hooray, another blackout!" said Tom delightedly.

"Here's your allowance for the next two weeks," Tom advanced.

"I'm here in your home for a visit," Tom guessed.

"I could use a pencil sharpener," said Tom bluntly.

"Shall I frost the birthday cake?" Tom offered icily.

"I just love adorable little bunnies," said Tom acutely.

"You have the right to remain silent," said Tom arrestingly.

"I totaled those up for you," Tom added.

"I want a hot dog," said Tom frankly.

"May I join your singing group?" Tom inquired.

"That's not *really* Dracula," Tom discounted.

"Hey, I am so not full of hot air!" Tom belched.

"I fixed the broken toilet!" proclaimed Tom, flushed with success.

"I can do that math really fast," said Tom calculatingly.

"Sure, there's room for one more," Tom admitted.

"I just got a job putting up steel girders!"
Tom beamed.

"Look out for that bird!" cried out Tom, ducking.

"Let's get married," Tom proposed engagingly.

"Hey, what's it worth to you if I can help you escape from prison?" asked Tom contemptuously.

"The train's late," Tom railed.

"I've spotted more blackbirds than you have," Tom crowed.

"Let's go shoot some hoops!" Tom bawled.

"I've got to fix the car," said Tom mechanically.

"I only want to hang out with ladies," Tom mentioned.

"Dawn came too soon," Tom mourned.

"I lost the debate when I ran out of things to say," said Tom outspokenly.

"The exit is right there," Tom pointed out.

"There's something missing from this flower bouquet," Tom said lackadaisically.

"Hurray for our sports team!" said Tom cheerfully.

"Fire!" bellowed Tom alarmingly.

"Hey, use your own hair brush!" Tom bristled.

"You snake!" Tom rattled.

"The eclipse is now starting," said Tom darkly.

"Now I can do some painting," said Tom easily.

"It's true, I chop down trees for a living,"
said Tom lumberingly.

"I'm a tailor," Tom panted.

"All right! I'm head of the refreshment committee!" said Tom, pleased as punch.

"Pete! Pete! Pete! Pete! Pete!" Tom repeated.

"This must be a spinning class," Tom worked out.

"Do I hear an echo?" was Tom's resounding question.

"That door is ajar," said Tom openly.

"You must draw the line somewhere," Tom ruled.

"Stop that horse!" cried Tom woefully.

THE JOKIEST JOKING PUNS BOOK EVER WRITTEN . . . NO JOKE!

Where do baby spoons come from?
The spork.

Why did the computer crash?

It had a bad driver.

What's loud, musical, and keeps sweat out of your eyes?

A headband.

What has four wheels and flies?

A garbage truck.

Why was the calendar out late Friday night?

It had a date!

I've never seen a fossil so opposed to doing any work.
Talk about a lazy bones!

How come the mail arrived wet?

There was postage dew.

What's a better name for a fly swatter?

A splatula!

I just read this novel in Braille.

It was a feel-good story.

That metal wire got so upset over some minor thing.

It got all bent out of shape over nothing!

How do space cowboys see in the dark?
Saddle lights.

Have you ever met that really funny sewing machine?

It keeps everyone in stitches.

What did the pencil say to the knife?

"You sure are looking sharp today!"

What did the paper say to the pencil?

"You have a good point."

It's time to sell your vacuum cleaner.

It's just gathering dust.

Why did the woodsman put on pajamas?
He was invited to a lumber party.

While it cost a lot of money at Halloween, that mask has no face value.

"Wow, look at that ceiling! What a great paint job! It's so high up there!"
–Ceiling fans

He didn't use to like masking tape.
Then he became very attached to it.

Who steals soap out of bathtubs?
A robber ducky!

When I came across that big pile of free pants on the street, I really picked up the slack.

I was going to buy some thin sandals to wear on my beach trip.
But then I flip-flopped.

What did the kid say when his math teacher gave him a yardstick?
"This rules!"

Why did Miss Muffet need a map?
Because she lost her whey.

The kid's pants zipper broke.
But he fixed it on the fly.

What's round and angry?
A vicious circle.

I didn't want to know that she had false teeth, but some things come out in conversation.

What do brooms say to each other at bedtime?

"Sweep tight!"

What's another name for a grandfather clock?

An old-timer.

What did the big bucket say to the little bucket?

"You look a little pail."

Why did the teddy bear turn down dessert?

Because he was stuffed.

A beautiful marble statue decided to move off of her perch. She was tired of being taken for granite.

Where does a power cord go shopping?

The outlet mall.

You should read this book about how boats are held together.

It was riveting.

A man went into a hardware store and asked to see some tools he could use to break up hard ground. The clerk took him to a wall of shovels, hoes, and other tools.

He says, "Take your pick."

The teacher quit their job teaching kids how to do origami. Too much paperwork.

My mom gave some old rope a time-out.

It was being very knotty.

Have you heard the joke about the roof?

Never mind, it's definitely over your head.

Did you hear the one about the unstamped letter?

Never mind, you won't get it.

What vitamin will sting you?
Vitamin B.

Want to hear a joke about paper?

Never mind, it's tearable.

Two houses situated next door to each other fell in love.

It was a lawn-distance relationship.

A nickel and a penny jumped off a moving train together.

But not the quarter. It had more cents.

"This job isn't for everyone," the scarecrow said, "but hay, it's in my jeans."

I call my alarm "Jim."
That way I can tell people the first thing I do every morning is hit the Jim.

"Boy," said one shelf to the other shelf, "you sure look board."

Your fingers are a lot like the hardware store.
They've both got a lot of nails.

How do "Stop," "Merge," and "Yield" signs communicate?
Sign language.

Telling puns in an elevator is just wrong on so many levels.

Where do boats go when they get sick?
To the dock.

You can have my chimney for free.
It's on the house!

Why did the beams get together once a week?
It was their support group.

Did you hear that metal and a microwave fell in love?
When they met, sparks flew!

I asked my friend, Nick,
if he had 5 cents I could borrow.
But he was Nicholas.

I bought a wooden whistle . . . but it wooden whistle.

What kind of shoes do ninjas wear?
Sneakers!

He couldn't work out how to fix the washing machine.

So he threw in the towel.

If you buy a bigger bed you actually get less bedroom.

These reverse-angle cameras in cars are great.

I got one and I never looked back.

The candle quit its job.

He felt burned out.

If you're looking for a rugged experience,
try traveling on a flying carpet.

My phone has to wear glasses.
Well, ever since it lost its contacts.

People say I look better without my glasses on.
But I just can't see it.

If artists wear Sketchers . . . then do linguists wear Converse?

I just read a book on anti-gravity.
I couldn't put it down!

My new diet consists entirely of aircraft.
It's a bit plane.

Why are there fences on graveyards?
Because people are dying to get in.

Remember: Models of dragons are not to scale.

I owe a lot to the sidewalks.
They've kept me off the streets for years.

How do you keep an ig from falling off?
Igloo.

Towels can't tell jokes.
They have a very dry sense of humor.

I thought this old rope would be useful, but nope—a frayed knot.

Never trust an escalator.
They're always up to something!

That poor piece of paper pinned up to the wall!
It was under a tack.

Why did the smelter get arrested?

For steeling the iron.

There's nothing more odd than numbers not divisible by two.

Do houses wear clothes?

Sure—a dress.

What do you call a belt with a watch on it?
A waist of time.

A broken can opener is really just a can't opener.

I'm sorry you got hit on my way into the room.
Honestly, I a-door you.

A woman came home to find she'd been robbed of every lamp in her house.
She was de-lighted.

Never leave your wooden shoes in the bathroom.
Otherwise people will think you clogged the toilet.

A man was walking through a quarry when he remarked, "Wow, what a big rock."

"Boulder," his friend said.

So he replied,

"Oh my goodness that's the MOST AMAZING ROCK I'VE EVER SEEN!"

There's a wash basin standing in front of your door right now.

Just let that sink in.

They could make pencils with erasers on both ends. But then, what would be the point?

Him: Does it seem weird that there's just one big factory that makes all the perfume in the world?
Her: Yeah, it makes scents.

Not only is a bride's last name new, she also gets a dress.

That table was so rude.
It said it couldn't chair less!

A girl brought a ladder to the first day of classes.
She thought she was starting high school.

How do you stop a baby spaceship from crying?
Rocket.

A belt was recently arrested.
It was caught holding up a pair of pants.

The mama toilet let her kid stay home from school one day.
She was looking a little flushed.

What did the hat say to the scarf?
"You can just hang around. I'll go on a head."

Never was there a more groundbreaking invention than the shovel.

Two of my friends always liked to sit right by the window.
Classic Kurt and Rod!

How come a bicycle can't stand up on its own?
It would, but it's two-tired.

Eating a clock may seem like a good idea, but keep in mind that it's very time consuming.

Have you picked up one of those brand-new state-of-the-art brooms?

Well, they're sweeping the nation!

I got a bump on my head because a book fell on it.

Sure, it hurts, but really, I only have my shelf to blame.

Two smartphones got married.

The wedding was a simple affair, but the reception was excellent.

What did one shirt say to the other?
"Meet me at the clothesline. It's where I hang out."

Did you hear about the guy who got a universal remote control?

He just held it in his hands and said, "This changes everything!"

One wind turbine met another wind turbine the other day and was very excited.

"What can I say?" it said. "I'm a big fan!"

Did you hear about the hungry clock?

It went back four seconds.

Person: "You ate the dictionary? Bad dog! Spit it up."
Dog: "You took the words right out of my mouth."

Girl: I used to have a terrible fear of hurdles.
Boy: What did you do?
Girl: I got over it.

The thing about whiteboards is that they're remarkable.

Did you hear about the girl who lost her watch?
She wanted to find it, but she didn't have the time.

I asked a tailor to make me a brand-new pair of pants.
He was happy to do it, or sew it seems.

Did you hear about the electronics shop downtown that's giving out dead batteries?
Yep, totally free of charge.

This one goes out to the guy who invented zero.
Thanks for nothing!

I got into the car the other day and I seemed to have forgotten how to buckle my seatbelt.
I struggled for a while until finally it clicked.

I really want to buy one of those new reversible jackets.

I'm excited to see how it turns out.

For some reason, my best friend left a ton of clay at my house.

I don't know what to make of it.

How do you make an hourglass run faster?

Fill it with quicksand.

If you have wrinkled clothing, it's certainly a pressing issue.

You'll need to iron out a solution.

This small sweater fits great, but it is hard to pull off.

Of all the jobs out there, being a mirror inspector is one I could really see myself doing.

Would you like to check out my mind-reading machine?

I'd love to hear your thoughts.

A guy walks into a restaurant and orders a meal.
He hears someone say,
"Hey, guy! Nice pants! Nice shirt! Great jacket!
Where did you get those amazing shoes?"
He looks around and realizes that there's nobody else around.
The waiter comes over and points to the bread basket.
"It's the rolls," he says. "They're complimentary."

I ordered a book of puns last week.
But I didn't get it.

6
EAT UP!

Here are some food puns to chew on . . . if you don't think they're too cheesy or corny.

There's only one way to fix a cracked pumpkin.
That's with a pumpkin patch.

What did the sesame seed say to the bagel?

"I'm on a roll!"

What's a good name for an almond in space?

An astronut!

A jar of pickles witnessed one of their own fall out of the fridge and onto the floor.

They just had to dill with it.

Take the edible part out of a couple of bananas and what do you have left? A pair of slippers.

The bagel was made from the fanciest flour and other ingredients.

It was well-bread.

What did one plate say to the other plate?

"Lunch is on me!"

The cool mushroom always got invited to all the best parties. Who doesn't love a fungi?

Did you hear about the sour orange that was expelled from school for being late?

The teacher got tired of how it was always tarty.

Newton's Law says what goes up must come down.

Cole's Law is thinly sliced cabbage with dressing.

Why do cowboys put big hats and boots on their salads?

They prefer ranch dressing.

What do you give a lemon that needs help?

Lemon-aid.

What did one hot dog say to the other hot dog in the hot dog race? "I relish the fact that you've mustard the strength to Ketchup to me!"

I smeared some ketchup all over my eyes once.

It was a bad idea in Heinz-sight.

Why did the pie see the dentist?

It needed a filling.

Want to hear one about an egg?

Never mind, you wouldn't get the yolk.

Today we ate a pizza on the roof of the pizza parlor.

The manager said it was on the house!

Yes, I'm into fitness.
Fitness whole burger in my mouth.

How do you make a tuna melt?

Pay it a nice compliment.

The scientist spit out her wad of gum when it ran out of flavor.

It was an ex-spearmint.

Boy: Have you ever eaten so many pintos and limas you get sick?

Girl: Yeah, I've bean there.

German sausages are the wurst.

Did you hear about the cat who fell into a pile of beans and wrapped itself up in a tortilla? It was a purr-ito.

Did you hear about the guy who got hit in the head with a flying can of soda?

He was just lucky that it was a soft drink.

My little sister told me there's no way that I could ever build a bicycle out of spaghetti.

You should've seen her face when I rode pasta.

Did you hear about the cracker that went to the hospital?

It was just feeling crummy.

What do you call an avocado with an electric guitar?
A guac star!

What nut are the most people allergic to?

Cashew!

Do you know why they sell sausages as links?

Because the butchers need to make ends meet.

There was a big sale at the fish market today.

Certainly there must be a catch!

There was once an army of pickles led by a brilliant pickle general.

It was a case of the brined leading the brined.

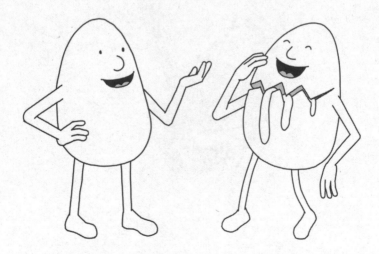

You don't hear eggs telling each other jokes much.
Otherwise, they'd crack up.

Boy: Some kid just came up to me and through a bunch of milk, cream, and cheese at me!

Girl: How dairy!

What's the difference between a pizza and pizza jokes?

Pizza jokes can't be topped!

Did you hear about the woman who quit her job at the doughnut factory?

She just got tired of the hole business.

Do you want to hear the poem I wrote about tortillas?
Actually, it's more of a wrap.

If you want to have a successful luau, you're going to have to go whole hog.

Did you hear about the guy who used to be a baker?
He enjoyed it, but he didn't make enough dough.

What do a weak cup of coffee and a cow that just gave birth have in common?
One is decaffeinated, and the other is de-calf-inated.

Did you hear about the block of cheese that went to the gym? It wanted to get shredded.

What do young Boy Scouts eat?

Cub sandwiches.

With all those pricklies on the outside, that one tropical fruit should be called a spineapple.

Why did they call it a salad bar, and not a veggie table?

What do a caramely candy bar and a cow's udder have in common?

They're both a Milky Way.

A not-very-smart kid ate his homework assignment. His teacher told him that it was a piece of cake.

You can eat a sandwich any time of day.

It's always a square meal.

Did you hear about the kid who dipped his iPhone in caramel?

He wanted a candied Apple.

How do you make a lemonade stand?

Steal the lemonade's chair.

Pirates always love hitting the farmer's market.
They love the corn, and the price is great:
a buck an ear!

Did you hear about the 1,000-pound wad of bubble gum?
It was positively chewmongous!

What do you call a jar of pickles so big that you can't fit it in the fridge?
Cucumbersome!

Did you hear about the kid who had to eat cold, lumpy mush for breakfast?
Now that's just gruel!

How do you make an egg roll?
Push it down a hill.

What do monsters eat for breakfast?

Scream of Wheat.

It was such a beautiful wedding, everyone was crying.

Even the cake was in tiers!

Farmer 1: These seeds still haven't sprouted yet!
Farmer 2: Don't worry. They'll turnip.

How do you make meatloaf?

Give it a big bag of chips and a Netflix account.

What do zombies put on their Thanksgiving turkey?

Grave-y.

What do vegetarian zombies eat?

"Graaaaaains!"

What should you eat to improve your vision?

Seafood!

Did you guys see the amazing movie about hot dogs?

It was an Oscar wiener.

What do you get when you cross fruit with a saxophone?

Jazzberries!

What kind of candy could you eat on the playground?

Recess Pieces.

It was a sell-out crowd at the potato hockey game.

The stands were full of spec-taters.

The cabbage won the big race.

In fact, it was a head the whole time.

Why did the dad put fruit in his coffee?
He was in the mood for brewberries.

Why did the hunter get arrested after making breakfast?

Because he poached his eggs.

Actual Restaurants With Funny Names

Wok This Way

Pita Pan

Look Into My Pies

Lord of the Fries

Lettuce Souprise You

Lettuce B. Frank

The Wiener's Circle

Nincomsoup

The Dairy Godmother

Cheesy Does It

Kale Me Crazy

Thai Tanic

Franks-a-Lot

Pastabilities

Aesop's Bagels

Basic Kneads Pizza

Turnip the Beat

Planet of the Crepes

Grillennium Falcon

Nothing Bundt Cakes

New Cod on the Block

Vincent Van Doughnut

Sconehenge

Frying Nemo

Udder Delights Cheese Cellar

Pony Espresso

Relish the Thought

Those students who went on a class field trip to the 7-Up factory . . .

should have known there would be a pop quiz.

Bananas never get lonely.
That's because they travel in bunches.

The kid burned her Hawaiian pizza.

She probably should have put the oven on aloha setting.

A family went on a tropical food diet. They ate nothing but fruit.

It's enough to make a mango crazy!

What's the best food to eat in the bathroom?

Showerkraut.

A tub of yogurt showed up to the art exhibit.
"What are you doing here?" a patron asked.
The yogurt replied, "I'm very cultured."

What do you get when you drop a book of nursery rhymes into a glass of O.J.?
Mother Juice!

Did you hear about the haunted pancake house?
That place gives me the crepes!

"That sure is a nice ham," the butcher said.
"It would be a shame if something put an 'S' on the front and an 'E' at the end."

How do you make a popsicle?
Let your dad fall through the ice!

A hamburger bun went to school and did so well that it made the honor roll.

Gosh, whoever invented Altoids must have made a mint!

Why was the racehorse named Creamy Orange?
Because he was a sherbet.

What would you call a beautiful pumpkin?
Gourd-geous!

How do you make a horse a sandwich?

With thoroughbred.

What hotel does cheese stay in?

The Stilton.

What kind of cheese can fly and go after its enemies?

Curds of prey.

How do you make sheep cheese?

Ewe's milk.

What kind of cheese is a lion's favorite?

Roar-quefort.

What cheese should you use to protect a castle?

Moat-zerella.

What did the cheese say after it heard a funny joke?

"Oh, that's a gouda one!"

What dance do cheesemakers do at Halloween?

The Muenster Mash.

You know what's so funny about egg jokes?
They crack me up!

A nut wanted to go to college.
It was interested in higher macademia.

Want to hear a pizza joke?
Never mind, it's too cheesy.

Name a vegetable that's awesome,
but not too awesome. The radish!

Never eat day-old sushi.
It's a little fishy.

Why did the cookie cry?
Because its father was a wafer so long!

I cut my finger chopping cheese.
I think that I may have grater problems.

If you didn't like that last cheese joke, you might be laugh-tose intolerant.

Did you hear about the magician who loved candy bars?
He had a couple of Twix up his sleeve.

Did you hear about the campers who left a big pot of beans, meat, and sauce on their grill?
It was chili outside.

I can't decide whether to make French toast or pancakes!
I keep waffling.

Why couldn't the chef finish making her famous spiced chicken?

She didn't have enough thyme.

Sometimes a root beer fizzes so loudly that it sounds like it's talking to me.

Soda speak.

What kind of nuts do your feet like?

Ca-shoes.

I just can't be friends with someone who doesn't eat pickles.

Sorry, but that's a dill-breaker.

What do sea monsters eat for lunch?

Fish and ships.

Did you hear about the shy vegetarian?

They avoided meet.

Why do eggs come in cartons?

So they don't eggscape.

Good soup is souper!

There is nothing worse than dried fruit in cookies.

And yes, I am being unraisinable!

There was jam stolen.

It was a strobbery!

Did you hear that old joke about cake?

It's pretty stale.

7
ON THE JOB

If you want to laugh at these jokes about jobs, well, you better get to work.

When you're named dentist of the year, they give you a reward. It's just a little plaque.

Did you hear about the woman who used to be a train driver?
She got sidetracked.

Never trust an acupuncturist.
First they needle you, and then they end up stabbing you in the back!

Can I fill you in on my trip to the dentist?

My molars are really bothering me. Good thing I have a dentist appointment today.
At 2:30.

Santa's best toy-making elf left the North Pole and started her own very successful toy company. Now she's extremely welfy.

Receptionist: Hello, please take a seat. The dentist will see you shortly.
Patient: Thank you, I'm familiar with the drill.

After the police caught the burglar, they poured cement on the culprit.
Now he's a hardened criminal.

Did you hear about the singer who got locked out of her house?
She broke into song and couldn't find the key.

After he quit pirating, the peg-legged pirate got a job waiting tables. At IHOP.

My grandfather is a baker, but he's never let me have his gingerbread recipe.

He said it's on a knead-to-know basis.

Did you hear about the pirate who covered his eye with sandpaper?

He was in a bit of a rough patch.

Pirates have a hard time getting through the alphabet.

They always get lost at C.

What did the pirate say when his wooden leg fell off during a snowstorm? "Shiver me timbers!"

Why didn't the pirate take a bath before he walked the plank?

Because he figured he'd wash up on shore later.

**"Yarr," said one pirate to another,
"what a nice wooden peg ye got thar. . . .
And such a shiny hook, too! How much did they cost?"**

The other pirate said, "An arm and a leg."

What's another name for a happy cowboy?
A jolly rancher!

What did the pirate say on his 80th birthday?

"Aye matey!"

Old carpenters don't retire.

They just lumber around.

If you're ever searching for a job, the trick is to look inside yourself.

Then, it's all about the inner view.

Did you hear about the skeleton comedian?
It was trying tibia little humerus.

What's the most tedious place in an office?

The bored room.

The pilot liked to be alone.

But even for him, flying a drone was just too remote.

What car would a farmer drive?

A cornvertible.

The failed poet decided to leave the writing to the prose.

What do you call a carnivore who also forecasts weather? A meat-eorologist.

We hired a tree trimmer and he did a great job.

He should take a bough!

What happened when the worker rotated the heavy machinery?

He got cranky.

I got fired from my job flipping burgers.

Apparently I didn't turn up enough.

After years of hard work on the subject, the excited scientist finally unlocked the secret to human cloning. He was beside himself!

My brother got a job making telescopes.

Things are looking up!

Did you hear about the barista who quit her job at the coffee shop?

She couldn't stand the daily grind.

I was supposed to do a list of odd jobs.

I finished numbers 1, 3, 5, 7, and 9.

I used to work as a hairdresser,
but I just wasn't cut out for it.

A witch published a book of all her potion recipes, but it was ultimately useless.

She'd forgotten to run a spell-check.

When construction workers party, they raise the roof!

The ship's captain was expected to dock in a very tiny little space. . . .

He was under a lot of pier pressure.

Why did the scarecrow get promoted?
Because he was outstanding in his field.

We hired a door-maker the other day.

She really knew how to make an entrance.

My new girlfriend tends to bees all day.

She's a keeper!

The fishing company had a very catchy slogan:

"Yes, we can!"

A man sued an airline company after it lost his luggage.

Unfortunately, he lost his case.

Why did the man dig a hole in his neighbor's backyard
and fill it with water? He meant well.

I was accused of being a plagiarist.

Their words, not mine.

The "old woman who lived in a shoe" wasn't the sole owner.

There were strings attached.

A persistent banker wouldn't stop bothering me.

So I asked him to leave me a loan.

I hear that the post office is a mail-dominated industry.

What does a fisherman magician say?
"Pick a cod, any cod!"

A doctor broke his leg while auditioning for a play.
Luckily, he still made the cast.

The balloon maker had to close down her business.
She couldn't keep up with inflation.

Government leaders don't engage in surfing contests. . . .
It could set a president.

Kid: How do you like your job?
Garbage Collector: It's picking up.

Electricians are the friendliest people on the planet.
They really know how to make good connections.

Why are kindergarten teachers so great?

They know how to make the little things count.

A scientist wanted to clone a deer.

So he bought a doe-it-yourself kit.

A man was fired from his job at the calendar factory.

Just because he took a couple of days off!

Barbers are excellent drivers.

They know all the shortcuts.

Why couldn't the lifeguard rescue the hippie?
He was too far out, man.

A ship carrying red paint shipwrecked.

It marooned all the sailors.

I know a tailor who doesn't mind making a pair of pants for me.

Or sew it seams.

I used to be a banker.

Until I lost interest.

Did you hear about the psychic with four heads?
They were a real four-chin teller.

Kitchen remodelers are very counterproductive.

A man heard that gold was discovered in Alaska. He immediately packed up his possessions and moved up there. Six months later, he gave up and went home. *It didn't pan out.*

They buried the man in the wrong place. *Talk about a grave mistake.*

Doctors are monitoring the condition of the boy who swallowed a handful of pennies, to see if he's passed them. No change yet.

This one police station lets criminals take their own
pictures. They call them cellfies.

How come the detective stayed in bed all day?
She was working undercover.

Patient: Doctor, my nose is running.
Doctor: I think it's not.

How do dog catchers get paid?
By the pound.

What do you call a student who always turns in their math homework late?
A calcu-later.

When the medieval warrior was awarded by the king, he was given a knighthood.
It was a big sir prize!

Policeman: Got any I.D.?
Lady: Got any I.D. about what?

How are actors going out on stage like little kids?
They like going to the play-ground.

I just produced a theatrical performance on puns.
It was a play on words.

8
HOW VERY ENTERTAINING

Movies, Music, and More

What's the funnest candy in the world?
An entertain-mint!

Why'd they name it "television"?

Because "watch" was already taken.

Elsa and Anna couldn't get any money out of their bank.

Their accounts had been frozen.

I can't believe the movie had a tornado at the end.

What a twist!

Congratulations to Gaston!

He won the No Belle Prize.

Let's all give a hand to these sock puppets!

Why was the Incredible Hulk such a good gardener?

He had a green thumb.

Why did the movie star put her house under a grove of citrus trees?

She wanted to live in the limelight.

What music does a balloon hate?

Pop.

There once was a poor actor who fell right through the floor during a performance. It was a stage he was going through.

Despite our hard work on our camping trip, we couldn't get the tent up.

Too many missed stakes.

Some parents don't let their kids watch orchestra performances on TV.

They say there's too much violins.

I came home today and my piano was sitting on the porch.

It forgot its keys.

Why did the boys fire their slingshots into the air?
They just wanted to shoot the breeze.

What's brown, wrinkled, and lives in a tower in France?

The lunch bag of Notre Dame.

The magician was driving down the street.

And then poof, he turned into a driveway.

Don't click the link in that guy's social media profile or you'll get a virus.

It's a bio-hazard.

A man threw every book in his vast library into the ocean. It started a title wave.

Books That Should Exist . . . And Who Should Write Them

Put on the Brakes *by Sloan Down*

Mountain Climbing Dangers *by Cliff Hanger*

Growing Your Own Spices *by Herb Garten*

Dare Ya! *by Hugo Furst*

Good Tries *by Ernest Steffert*

I Bet You Enjoyed It *by Major Day*

Are Your Parents Doing Well? *by Howard DeFolks*

How to Be a Dog *by Ima K. Nine*

What do skeletons play in the band?
The trombone.

The Most *by Max E. Mumm*
The Least *by Minnie Mumm*
We're Not Done Here *by Morris Cumming*
Cooking with Shortening *by Chris Coe*
Playing with Fireworks *by Huell B. Sourry*
Riding a Horse Without a Saddle *by Eiffel Downe*
How to Identify Cattle *by Brandon Iron*
How to Sing *by Mel O'Dee*
Dinnertime on the Ranch *by Dean R. Bell*
When Life Is Boring *by Dulles Dishwater*
Unpredictable Situations *by Mayer Mayknott*

Why do dust bunnies use computers?
To get on the linternet.

The Story of Archery *by Bowen Narrow*

How to Make Fried Food *by Crispin Brown*

My Life as a Singer *by Mimi Mee*

Earrings *by Pierce Stears*

Census Methods *by Harmony Arthur*

Trick Airplane Flying *by Lupe de Loop*

Be Prepared *by Justin Case*

Jobs for Kids *by Hiram Young*

How to Get Your Blood Taken *by Amos Skeeto*

The Exploding Man *by Stan Wellback*

Hereditary Allergy Symptoms *by Constance Niffling*

What kind of warts would you find on a space frog?
Star Warts.

The Heavy Load *by Aiken Back*
Demolition Derby *by Rex Carrs*
Stop Fidgeting *by Stan Still*
The Baker's Man *by Pat E. Cake*
Extra Innings *by Willy Won; Illustrated by Betty Wont*
The Worst Joke Book Ever *by Terry Bull*

That movie about the colander wasn't very good.
The plot had too many holes. I was straining to understand it.

What music does a mummy like best?
Wrap.

Ever since he went to Neverland, Peter Pan just wouldn't stop flying around.

How did Darth Vader know what Luke was getting him for his birthday?
He could sense his presents.

Why was Dr. Frankenstein's assistant so enthusiastic to help?
He was just Igor!

What music does a boulder like best?
Rock.

How does Clark Kent keep the sun out of his eyes when he's flying around as his heroic alter ego?

A supervisor.

What does Superman like in his drinks?

Just ice.

Why does Superman get invited to lots of dinner parties?

Because he's a supperhero.

I just ate a bunch of Scrabble tiles.
My next trip to the bathroom could spell disaster.

I don't care for Russian nesting dolls.
They're so full of themselves.

Have you ever tried going to bed with music playing?
It will give you sound sleep.

The show is called *SpongeBob SquarePants*, but everyone knows the star was Patrick.

Did you hear about the human cannonball?
It's too bad he got fired!

You can have these marionettes, free of charge.
Honestly, no strings attached.

Breaking news: Cartoonist lost in the woods. . . .
Details are sketchy.

Did you hear that they opened a restaurant on the moon?
The food was great, but there was no atmosphere.

News anchor: This just in: I'm holding a boat to a dock.

Never go fishing with a DJ.
They always drop the bass.

There's a new drama series coming on TV next week starring a pair of pliers.

I hear it's very gripping.

I like fairy tales, but some of them have a tendency to dragon.

Not many people watch *Dumbo* anymore.

That movie is increasingly irrelephant.

A woman stole a saxophone.
Police charged her with grand theft alto.

Humpty-Dumpty may have had a miserable summer.
But hey, he had a great fall.

What happened when the guy dropped a piano into a mineshaft?
A flat miner.

Wile E. Coyote didn't go out and chase the Road Runner today.
He had a bad case of Acme.

Put your grandma on speed dial.
Boom: Insta-Gram!

Who recorded all the exploits of the Knights of the Round Table for history?

King Author.

Did you see that movie about punctuation?

It was a period piece.

It's very hard to get a reservation at the library.

They're always totally booked!

There was a fire at the circus, and gosh, it was in tents.

The king's official comedian sent me a birthday card.
Now, wasn't that a nice jester?

You know why Waldo always wear stripes?

That way he won't be spotted.

Mickey Mouse helped his girlfriend buy a car.

She picked out a nice Minnie van.

Gosh, when my parents found out that I'd replaced their bed with a trampoline, they just about hit the roof.

Have you ever had a Chewbacca steak?

It's a little Chewy.

Did you know that Dracula gets really bad allergies in the spring? That's why they call him the Pollen Count.

What's Batman's favorite sandwich?

Reuben.

Did you hear that Dracula was named the best bloodsucker of the year?

What a champire!

The Invisible Man tried to lie to me, but I saw right through him.

Have you heard that scary story about the haunted freezer? It's chilling!

Why does Godzilla rampage through the city and eat hotel rooms?

He has a suite tooth.

Did you know there's a 007 who spies only underwater?

James Pond!

Have you read the book about teleportation?

It's bound to get you somewhere.

I used to think I wanted to become a mime, but then I didn't think it sounded very good.

Bad Guy: Gimme your guitar! I'm going to rip every piece off of it!

Good Guy: Oh yeah? Is that a fret?

Before he fought crime, Batman was a pastry chef.

They called him the Crepe Crusader!

Did you know Batman was also a butcher?

It was when he lived in Got-Ham.

Did you hear that Simba put on a tuxedo?

He was a real dandy-lion.

When is a novel also a short story?

When it's The Hobbit.

All jokes about Peter Pan are good because they never get old.

9
THE REAL WORLD

Life, the world, and everything in it can be kind
of punny sometimes.

What's a good name for a guy who
works at a gas station? Phil!

Real Names of Hair Salons

Headmasters

Mane Attraction

Fort Locks

Shear Delight

Fresh Hair

Shear Madness

Blade Runners

Alive and Klippin'

Hair and Now

Hairoglyphics

Hair Necessities

Tortoise & The Hair

The Hairport

Cutting Remarks

The Mane Event

Cut 'N' Run

Curl Up and Dye

Hair On Earth

Headgames

Hair Today, Gone Tomorrow

Hair Raisers

Scissors Palace

Hairanoia

Politicians with Amusing Names

Janelle Lawless was a circuit court judge in Michigan.

Jay Walker ran for office in Pierce County, Georgia.

Dave Obey was a congressman from Wisconsin.

Timothy Shotwell ran for a sheriff position in Clark County, Washington.

Krystal Ball ran for office in Virginia in 2010. She didn't win . . . but she probably should have seen that coming.

What's a good name for a kid who lives
in the bathroom? John!

Funny Beach House Names

Latitude Adjustment

Once Upon a Tide

Sea-Esta

What's Up Dock

Shore Thing

Family Tides

Beachy Keen

All Decked Out

What's a good name for a firefighter?
Ashley!

Sand Castle
Gimme a Break
Surf 'n' Sound
Dune Our Thing
Shore Fun
Seaclusion
Sunny Daze
Hide 'n' Sea
A Wave From It All
Wait 'n' Sea
Baywatch
Something Fishy

What's a good name for somebody who does yoga?
Matt!

When it comes to delivering her dialogue well, Anne Hathaway with words.

Which pop star makes rapid onstage wardrobe changes?
Tailor Swift.

Can you talk to your phone and ask it to do stuff?
No Siri.

What do you call a lady with a frog on her head?
Lily!

What's a good name for a person with a car on their head?

Jack!

What's a good name for a lady who wears a lot of red?

Scarlett!

What's a good name or someone who plays a stringed instrument?

Harper!

What's a good name for a girl who lives on the moon? Luna!

What's the difference between Christopher Columbus
and the lid of a dish? One is a discoverer,
the other is a dish coverer.

Syncing....

I changed my iPhone name to Titanic.
It's syncing now.

Truly there was no one in history who traveled and wandered around more than the Romans.

What do surfers wash their swim trunks in?
Tide.

A kid thought he was swimming in an ocean made out of orange soda.
It turns out it was just a Fanta sea.

What's a good name for someone who plays the flute? Piper!

Velcro is such a rip-off!

What's better in an emergency than an EMT?
A pair-a-medics.

Why did they call it the Dark Ages?
Because there were so many knights.

What's a good name for a tall girl?
Willow!

There was a robbery at the Apple Store, but they caught the guy because of an iWitness.

I, for one, like Roman numerals.

Why does the singer of "Chandelier" not want us to Sia?

Who is the sleepiest world leader in history?
Nap-oleon.

Einstein developed a theory about space.

And it was about time, too.

Every car that isn't an Acura is technically an Inacura.

Paul Revere always carried tissues.
He was, after all, the town crier.

What does Adele eat for dessert?

Jell-O.

How did Adele treat her sunburn?

Aloe.

What did Benjamin Franklin say when he discovered electricity? "I'm shocked!"

When the apple hit him on the head, Sir Isaac Newton understood the gravity of the situation.

Did you know that a chimp was once the president? Ape-braham Lincoln!

How much does a hipster weigh?
An Insta-gram.

I was trying to take a picture when my friend
ran up and slathered Vaseline on my camera.
Now that's what I call a photo balm!

10
EARTH DAZE

Are these jokes about trees, flowers, and the living world bound to make you groan? Hey, it's only natural!

A's are a lot like flowers.
Bees follow them.

Did you hear about the belly button?

It was so smart that it went to school at the Navel Academy.

Did you hear the joke about the virus?

Never mind, I don't want to spread it around.

What's unthinkable?

An itheberg.

What part of a flower can power a bicycle?
The petals.

Why do trees make such terrible enemies?
Because they're the best at throwing shade!

Do you want a brief explanation of an acorn?
It's an oak tree, in a nutshell.

First Kid: Did you know that I can cut down a dead tree just by looking at it?
Second Kid: I know. I saw it with my own eyes!

The campfire was nearly dying, but now it's roaring again. "I'm stoked!" the fire said.

What month do trees dread?

Sep-timber!

Take it from a scientist:

Never believe atoms. They make up everything.

The tree was very successful.

So much so that it opened up lots of branches.

The trees were more than glad when fall and winter had both passed.

In fact, they were re-leafed.

What did the trees wear to the forest pool party?
Swimming trunks.

There's no real way to tell if someone is color-blind.
There's a lot of gray area.

I'd tell you a chemistry joke, but I know I wouldn't get a reaction.

Groups of really intelligent trees tend to grow next to each other.
It's called a brainforest.

If you think it's bad when it's raining cats and dogs, you should try hailing taxis.

What kind of trees do you get when you plant kisses?
Tulips.

What did the right eye say to the left eye?

"Between you and me, something smells."

They had a funeral for some boiled water.

It will be mist.

The clouds in the sky got so excited that it was spring that they wet their plants!

What's the best way to start a fire?

That's a subject that has been hotly debated.

Two flowers decided to grow next to each other.
After all, they were buds!

No two people interpret colors the exact same way.

In fact, it's a pigment of your imagination.

Some astronomers were supposed to watch the moon rotate for 24 whole hours.

But then they got bored and called it a day.

How do trees access the internet?

They log on.

There's nothing like a meteor shower
to rock your world.

During the middle of a heat wave, our town got dumped with snow.

The weatherman says it was an ice-olated incident.

The earth's rotation really makes my day.

Only one large petal remained on the old rose.

Last bud not least!

Why did the tonsils get all dressed up?
Because they heard a doctor was taking
them out tonight!

Why are trees such big sports fans?

They just like to root!

What did the cowboy say when the varmint gave him flowers?

"What in carnation?"

Gardeners hate weeds.

That's because if you give them an inch, they'll take a yard.

How do florists make money?

By petaling their goods.

How do big mountains in cold areas stay warm in the winter? Because they're topped with snowcaps.

Why didn't the scientist give her mother flowers on her birthday?

She hadn't botany!

What's the top prize at a flower show?

A bloom ribbon!

I now know how gemstones are made.

The process is crystal clear!

Gardeners love their work.
Going to their job everyday is like a bed of roses!

Trees hate taking tests.

Those questions always stump them!

Trees are living things, and they get sleepy, too.

They occasionally need a nap—forest.

The nose was feeling very sad.

It was so tired of getting picked on.

People using umbrellas always seem
to be under the weather.

There was a big natural disaster the other day.
The earthquake took the blame, saying "it was my fault."

Why did the piece of coal turn into a diamond?
It just couldn't take the pressure.

Why do geologists like their area of study so much?
It rocks!

In order for a fungus to grow, you have to give it as mushroom as possible.

A lot of people have big noses, but a nose cannot be longer than 12 inches. If it was, it would be a foot.

If you want to make some money, get into flower sales.

Business is blooming!

Most people prefer the summer to the winter.

And yet, snow happens weather you like it or not.

How do meteorologists greet each other?

With a heat wave!

There's only one tree that can fit in your hand.
A palm tree.

How do clouds salute the president?

They hail to the chief!

The weather forecast called for freezing rain today.

And sure enough, it was an ice day.

Do you think plant puns are funny?

We're fern believers!

The moon saves money by cutting its own hair.
How? Eclipse it.

During allergy season, it's best to wake up early and get all that snot out of your nose at once.
Sneeze the day!

Never discuss infinity with a mathematician.
They can go on about it forever.

What's the best way to impress an orchid?
Use lots of flowery language.

How come the little kid's tooth fell out?
Because it was looth.

If you live in an igloo, there's snow place like home.

11
GOOFING UP

We thought we "odd" to end this book on something silly.

Whenever you lie on the floor,
does it ever feel like the whole world is against you?

Do I have a time machine? . . . Of course I have a time machine . . . .

I've had one for a long time . . . .

We go way back.

What school subject is the most shaping?

Geometry!

There was no reason why my glasses suddenly fogged up. I was mystified!

I've memorized 25 letters of the alphabet.

I don't know Y.

I woke up this morning in the dark and forgot what happens next.

Then, it dawned on me.

Ed's parents named his brother Ed, too.
Because two Eds are better than one.

No, I don't want to go shopping with you.

Once you've seen one shopping center, you've seen a mall.

People who shed pounds are a bunch of losers.

I'm afraid that my fear of moving stairs isn't getting any better.

If anything, it's escalating.

A man checked into the hospital covered in hay and riding a horse. Doctors say he's in stable condition.

Boy: I haven't slept for ten days.
Girl: Well, good! That would be far too long.

It seemed like Santa would be late this year, but he arrived in the Nick of time.

What do elves learn in school?
The elf-abet.

A man went to buy some camouflage clothes.
He couldn't find any.

A girl went home to find a friend lying on her doorstep.
She said, "Oh, hi, Matt."

Did you hear about the mind-reading kid who robbed a bank and escaped?

There's a small medium at large!

Did you hear about the kid who wouldn't nap?

She was arrested for resisting a rest.

What birthday is your shortest?

Your twenty-second birthday.

A girl ran around and around her bed.
"What are you doing?" her concerned mother asked.
"I'm trying to catch up on my sleep."

Car repair should be called "autocorrect."

Don't tell jokes about being lazy. They just don't work.

Do you know sign language?
You should learn it, it's pretty handy.

The prices on these cat foods.
They're meowtrageous!

The future, the present, and the past walked into the room.

Things got a little tense.

Why don't some couples go to the gym?

Because some relationships don't work out.

What do you mean June is over?

Julying!

I was in the statue wing of the museum not paying attention when SMACK—I hit the rear-end of one. That was when I hit rock bottom.

The alien spacecraft crash landed on Earth in an office supply store.

Finally, a UFO caught on tape!

I met some aliens from outer space.

They were pretty down to earth.

What's it called when you have too many aliens?

Extraterrestrials.

Why is a skeleton a bad liar?
You can see right through it!

I had a pun about misplacement.

And then I lost it.

Why couldn't the dead car drive into the cluttered garage?

Lack of vroom.

Want to hear a pun about ghosts?

That's the spirit!

How can you tell a vampire has a cold?
By his coffin.

I really look up to my tall friends.

Q: What's the difference between a stamp and a girl?
A: One is a mail fee, and the other is a female.

This kid I knew was obsessed with monorails.
All he ever talks about is monorails,
particularly how they travel along a single rail.
He has a one-track mind!

What do you get if you cross a shaggy dog with a
vegetable? Collie-flower.

I never thought I wanted a brain transplant.

But then I changed my mind.

Did you hear the joke about the town dump?

Never mind, it's garbage.

Who is bigger, Ms. Bigger or her baby?

Well, the baby is a little Bigger.

What do you get when you cover a boat in slime?

An ooze cruise!

Did you hear the one about the dirty gym socks?
It stinks!

Why couldn't the kids go see the new pirate movie?

Because it was rated "arrrrrgh."

How long would it take you to count to infinity four times?

Four ever.

The cheapest way to travel is by sale boat.

Skeletons are great learners.
They always have an open mind.

Why did the man use the sauna?

He needed a boost of self a-steam.

Why'd they call them "self-driving vehicles"?

Because "automobile" was already taken.

We all went to the reading of the will and found out what we inherited.

It was a dead giveaway.

What did the woman's friends wish her before her staycation? "Non voyage!"

THE JOKIEST JOKING PUNS BOOK EVER WRITTEN . . . NO JOKE!

What kind of dog drives a sleigh and comes once a year?

Santa Paws.

The cardiovascular system is a work of artery.

However, it's also pretty vein.

She had a photographic memory . . . but she never developed it.

The man loved himself so much he bought a lot of mirrors. He used the self-checkout.

Never spell "part" backwards.

It's a trap!

Did you read that article on ancient Japanese warriors?

If not, I can samurais it.

What rhymes with orange?

No, it does not.

Did you hear about the two boats that were in love?
They had a wonderful relationship!